30 Days to
Your Next Level

BOB DONNELL

DEDICATION

This book is dedicated to:

My mom. Who, while only on this earth for the first 17 years of my life, demonstrated more to me about selflessness, patience, joy, love, and commitment than any other person. You were and are amazing in my life mom, and I love and miss you.

My kids: Brittney, Justin and Macy. You have all taught me so much about life, friendships, love, and, most importantly, about myself. Thank you for being who you are in my life and for allowing me the honor of being your dad. I love you each.

Cindy Vaughn. You are one of the finest human beings I have ever met in my life. Your ability to adapt, take responsibility, always striving to be the best version of yourself, and be so forgiving, loving, kind and look for the good in every person and situation is greatly appreciated and admired.

CONTENTS

ACKNOWLEDGMENTS

This book would not be possible without the numerous mentors, coaches, friends and colleagues I have now and have had throughout the years.

People like: Tony Robbins, Les Brown, Keith Ferrazzi, Brian Tracy, Thomas Bahler, Jay Carty, Stephen Covey, Garth Brooks, Tim McGraw, Will Smith, Dr. Phil, Joel Osteen, Dr. David Cook, Dr. Bill Janeshak, Les Brown, and Jim Collins.

Special thanks to:

Wesley Goo. My friend, colleague and brother! Trainer of speakers and influence extraordinaire.

James S. Rutherford who, when told that I was publishing this book, said, "It's about time."

Glenn Morshower who inspires, delights, and shines in all he does!

AUTHOR'S NOTE

"We are not lacking information. What we lack is the implementation of the information which we already have."
Bob Donnell

This being said, here are some guidelines that will help you get the very most out of the strategies shared within this book. Your journey is now beginning in a new direction. I have spoken to countless numbers of people over the last 20 years and have found more often than not they absorb the information shared and then simply move on. I am committed to providing the opportunity for permanent change in people's lives by not only giving them inform-ation but also the structure, guidelines and tools necessary to help them implement the information they receive.

This book is a compilation of six weeks (five days within each week) of strategies that, when acted upon in the format given, **will create lasting change!**

I recommend you take the time to begin each week by:

1. Hand-writing the weekly strategy on a 3x5 card

2. Carrying it with you all week

3. Writing each day the action steps given on the back of the card

4. Taking action each day in the direction of which you'd like to be

It is my sincere desire that you begin to live a life by

design, rather than infliction of the circumstances of life!

Please email me at Admin@NextLevelLive.com and let me know of your journey!

Bob Donnell
Bob@NextLevelLive.com
www.NextLevelLive.com

Week 1

"I like to put myself into a position where I am choking my guts out to see just how good I can really be."

This was a quote from Dr. David Cook's discussion with a pro-golfer. Dr. Cook is an author and a speaker. This was from *The Mindset of a Champion*. I highly recommend it. It is available on CD. Let me know and I will find it for you.

Day 1

"I like to put myself in a position where I am choking my guts out to see just to see how good I can really be."

Dr. David Cook

I like the quote because it stresses the importance of pushing and expanding ourselves, so that we grow. There are far too many salespeople in this world just coasting, relying on past clients to keep them afloat, and waiting for the next "wave" of business. I like this topic because it says that even if we are "successful," are we really, if we haven't become all that we were intended to be?

Take Action

When was the last time you felt stretched? When was the last time you really grew? Sometimes we stop growing in stature and we take it as a cue that we are to stop growing in other areas as well... not so.

What is the most difficult thing you have attempted of late and what was the outcome? Was there growth?

Look for ways to grow in one or more of the following areas:

-Mentally

-Spiritually

-Emotionally

-Economically

-Relationally

-Physically

_____

_____

_____

_____

_____

_____

_____

_____

_____

_____

_____

_____

_____

_____

_____

_____

Day 2

"I like to put myself in a position where I am choking my guts out to see just to see how good I can really be."

Dr. David Cook

Well, are you choking yet? What things have you done to challenge yourself this week that are really stretching you? Growth comes from stretching. I have gotten feedback from some people saying they are working on stretching themselves in relationship building with clients, and others saying they are stretching themselves in the mode of work ethics; yet others are talking of stretching themselves in the area of making more qualified prospecting call, and the list goes on. What are you working on this week? I really want to know.

Take Action

Make just one or two more prospecting calls than you normally do. Remember, start with something small, get a success or two under your belt and you will be better able to handle the next phase.

Take an extra 15-30 minutes to read, listen to, or study something positive and get personal development as a habit for every day.

Make 5 phone calls to past clients today just to reconnect. Just say "Hi," don't talk about business unless they ask.

_____

_____

_____

_____

_____

_____

_____

_____

_____

_____

_____

_____

_____

_____

_____

_____

_____

Day 3

"I like to put myself in a position where I am choking my guts out to see just to see how good I can really be."

Dr. David Cook

How is this week turning out to be different than any other? Well, hopefully you are pushing yourself a little bit more each day to be better and better. What areas are you pushing yourself in?

Have you seen any improvement? Have you noticed any growth? Keep in mind the old fables about watching water boil or watching yourself grow in height. Sometimes what we are not able to see, those around us are taking note of and admiring. Sometimes, they notice from afar.

I am confident that as we seek to grow and expand in our experiences, we will grow to be better people, better friends, better colleagues, better husbands, better wives, you name it.

I want you to know I am proud to be on this journey with you and that I count it my privilege to be your "coach" as well as your friend!

_____

_____

_____

_____

_____

_____

_____

_____

_____

_____

_____

_____

_____

_____

_____

_____

_____

_____

Day 4

"I like to put myself in a position where I am choking my guts out to see just to see how good I can really be."

Dr. David Cook

Some are pushing themselves and some are not. Let me ask you something... If you are not pushing yourself beyond the norm this week, why not?

Are you afraid of failure? Are you afraid of success? Are you afraid of being uncomfortable? Whatever the reason, we must each overcome this challenge of complacency or not wanting to be uncomfortable.

I can think of a lot of things that would be more uncomfortable then making a few more phone calls, knocking on a few more doors, writing a few more notes, going to a few more social events, etc. C'mon, the decision is yours, start pushing yourself to do even just a little bit more. The reward will be incredible!

Take Action

Is there a past client you have been thinking about? Call them.

Is there an area where you really want to grow (spiritual, mental, emotional, physical fitness), then start right now. Spend 15-30 minutes just learning, and growing.

Is there a local social event that you have been thinking about attending to meet some new people?

Then go, put it in your calendar and go.

_____

_____

_____

_____

_____

_____

_____

_____

_____

_____

_____

_____

_____

_____

_____

_____

_____

Day 5

"I like to put myself in a position where I am choking my guts out to see just to see how good I can really be."

Dr. David Cook

Is anyone choking? I hope that what you have done this week was to find some ways to push yourself a bit further and to put the odds in your favor for increasing your life and your business!

I want to commend those of you that have stretched and forced yourself to do something uncomfortable because I know you are growing and are becoming the you that you were intended to be. Congrats and keep it up!

Sometimes the greatest gift we can give to ourselves is growth. Mental, physical, spiritual, business, relational, etc., these are all areas of great opportunity, but it will take growth in order to realize our full potential, and oftentimes growth is neither easy nor comfortable.

Take Action

Once you began to feel uncomfortable, did you stop or did you push on? In those areas that you stopped, go back and see if you can push through that barrier this weekend.

How many relationships did you enhance this week?

How many relationships did you begin this week?

Do you feel like you grew?

What kind of effect did this exercise have on your business this week?

_____

_____

_____

_____

_____

_____

_____

_____

_____

_____

_____

_____

_____

_____

_____

Week 2

"Be courageous! Whatever setbacks America has encountered, it has always emerged as a stronger and more prosperous nation…"
"Be brave as your fathers before you. Have faith and go forward."

Day 6

"Be courageous! Whatever setbacks America has encountered, it has always emerged as a stronger and more prosperous nation..." "Be brave as your fathers before you. Have faith and go forward."

Thomas Alva Edison

I called Sarah Caldicott (the great grandniece of Thomas Edison) this last week and I found myself in a rare situation. I have been fortunate and blessed enough to meet celebrities and famous people from all walks of life. I have never felt what I am about to describe so please bear with the awkwardness of describing it.

While Sarah and I were talking, I went to address the principle of the week and as I did, I found it very uncomfortable to call Mr. Edison, 'Thomas.' I found myself referring to him as 'Mr. Edison' over and over again. This struck me as odd since I don't feel awkward calling Donald Trump, Donald Trump, Lee Iacocca, Lee Iacocca, or anyone else any differently than their name.

During his life, Thomas encountered struggles, frustration, poor economics, and many of the same hardships that we see today. What inspired him to pen the above? Not sure, but one thing I know is that he was a man of hope and desired others to have hope in the future. What he created over his life time opened doors that many thought were welded shut, but through his determination the doors were not only opened, but were blown off the hinges and new opportunities arose!

This is such a great statement for America of yesterday, today and tomorrow! He makes a strong and determined command... "BE COURAGEOUS!" This economy, this time in history, and the opportunities presented require courage! It is not for the weak or easily intimidated. What we are facing is not going to be handed to us without effort on our part, but it is available to us. So many times in history, industries and individuals have been at a crossroads. This is such a time. The world is not lacking weak, easily intimidated, and un-resourceful people. What we lack are people that will stand tall- unyielding and courageous people!

Take Action

Look up the word courageous in an online dictionary. Then identify someone that you know to be courageous and explain why they define the word "courageous" for you by posting a comment to this blog.

_____

_____

_____

_____

_____

Day 7

"Be courageous! Whatever setbacks America has encountered, it has always emerged as a stronger and more prosperous nation…" "Be brave as your fathers before you. Have faith and go forward."

Thomas Alva Edison

Did you identify someone that you thought exemplified the word "courageous"?

Several people told me that as soon as they read the word, someone popped into their mind. If you did not do the exercise, go back and do it. The exercises are meant to take no more than a few minutes each day, yet provide a lifetime of results.

The next part of the principle is "Whatever setbacks America has encountered," I love this part because I believe for someone to be successful they will more often than not have to have a "whatever it takes, whatever obstacles come my way" attitude. America has faced many challenges and oppositions over the years. Today's families, businesses, communities and countries are facing some old and some new opponents. The mindset has to be that of whatever it takes. We as individuals, we as leaders, we as entrepreneurs, we as family partners need to rally behind the strategies that have proven successful for people, economies, and our great country. We must stand tall, face the winds of change and then be determined to weather the storm!

Take Action

Write the following on a 3x5 card and carry it with you the remainder of the week:

"I,_____, am determined to be the best that I can be, to encourage others to do the same and support those that are.

I am making it known that I am committed to the outcome I envision for myself, my family and my business. I will do whatever it takes, regardless of setbacks, to make my vision my reality!"

_____

_____

_____

_____

_____

_____

_____

_____

_____

_____

_____

Day 8

"Be courageous! Whatever setbacks America has encountered, it has always emerged as a stronger and more prosperous nation..." "Be brave as your fathers before you. Have faith and go forward."

Thomas Alva Edison

Are you determined and committed to succeed "no matter what"? I hope so. Reflect on that card you wrote yesterday.

Today we focus on "It has always emerged as a strong and more prosperous nation." Isn't it interesting that we go through so many challenges and it is only when we look back upon them that we realize the purpose of those challenges. They prepared us for something down the road. I look at my life and find so many instances in which, at the time, I thought were destined to destroy me, yet, looking back I find that they made me stronger. Being committed to "No matter what" allows you to deal with and grow through tough times. It does not keep the tough times from happening, but rather, it allows for growth and the ability to come out stronger and better for having gone through the tough times.

Are you going to be better and stronger for having gone through the challenges of your past, present and future? It will depend on your commitment level to that outcome. Your commitment level to being better will have to be bigger than your commitment to live life by infliction.

Take Action

On a scale of 1-10, what is your commitment level to living a life by design rather than infliction, and coming out of any circumstance bigger and better? When people meet you this week, will they see that commitment level in your stride, your confidence, your demeanor and your attitude?

_____

_____

_____

_____

_____

_____

_____

_____

_____

_____

_____

_____

_____

Day 9

"Be courageous! Whatever setbacks America has encountered, it has always emerged as a stronger and more prosperous nation…" "Be brave as your fathers before you. Have faith and go forward."

Thomas Alva Edison

The outcome we all want is to be stronger and more prosperous, isn't it?

I have found that most people are looking to be better and better off after any event in their life. Unfortunately, the desired outcome is more often than not overshadowed by the challenges we are facing.

I am facing a heart procedure as I write this and if they could guarantee that it would fix my heart, I would be very happy. But there are no guarantees. I have found over and over again that every situation I have encountered- the death of my mom, my being in a coma and a wheelchair for 7 weeks, and even the death of my daughter, Macy- gave me the opportunity to become a stronger and better person. Notice I said "opportunity," I did not say that they made me a better person, but rather the opportunity was granted by going through those events, and when I utilized them to my benefit, I benefited and so did those around me as they faced tough times in their lives.

The opportunity to become stronger is offered in the

experience, and yet so many will choose to hold on to the sadness of the events and allow it to break them into pieces and become less rather than more.

Take Action

Write the following on a 3x5 card today and carry it today and read it often:

No event will ever determine my attitude or my destiny. I am 100% in charge of both of them and it is up to me to become better by seizing the opportunity to become so.

_____

_____

_____

_____

_____

_____

_____

_____

_____

_____

_____

_____

Day 10

"Be courageous! Whatever setbacks America has encountered, it has always emerged as a stronger and more prosperous nation…" "Be brave as your fathers before you. Have faith and go forward."

Thomas Alva Edison

"Be brave as your fathers before you. Have faith and go forward." Wow! So much in so few words! What does it mean to be brave? Did it say, "be brave unless it's a health issue, it's a financial issue, it's a relational issue, it's a big issue?" No. It said "Be brave." Again the "no matter what" is inferred. Determining what brave means is the interesting part. Bravery to me is standing tall and pressing on in spite of what the negative consequences may be.

When I was 15 and in high school, my mom (and only known parent) was diagnosed with cancer and given 6 months to live. I remember her smile and her laugh and yet never once remember her complaining, saying, "woe is me!", or being angry about the cards dealt. Instead, I noticed her generosity and willingness to be kind and listen to other's problems frequently.

She used to say that she watched soap operas (Days of Our Lives was her favorite), so she could feel like her life was pretty darn good. She raised my two older brothers and me without even $1 of child support, and as a result we were forced to move due to no rent and did not have anything to speak of. But I never remember being hungry and I never remember her being upset about it. She was brave, no matter what.

I remember even as the cancer was taking her life, she never was afraid of dying. She was disappointed that she would not be around to see me graduate high school, meet my wife, or see my kids. That was Brave. She was afraid for how I was going to get through high school more than she was about losing her life.

Take Action

Who stands out in your mind as brave? Write them a note (even if deceased) and tell them thank you for setting the example for you and promise to live up to it in memory of them, no matter what! And then just have faith and go forward!

_____

_____

_____

_____

_____

_____

_____

_____

_____

Week 3

"I've had my moments, days in the sun. Moments I was second to none… Moments when I knew I did what I thought I couldn't do."

Emerson Drive
Moments

Day 11

**"I've had my moments, days in the sun
Moments I was second to none…
Moments when I knew I did what I thought I
couldn't do."**

Emerson Drive, *Moments*

Our lives are made up of moments. Where you are today is a direct result of the combination of those moments. Those moments, some good and some not so good, are compiled together and help to form who we are, what we are and how we are. It is not so much the moments themselves, as the way in which we decide to act upon those moments.

More often than not we can easily recall a negative thing said to us, or a negative event in our life, while at times we may have difficulty recalling something positive unless it was huge (i.e.: the birth of a child, your wedding day, etc.). It is imperative that the moments be translated (framed) correctly so that we receive the maximum benefit from each of them. You see, the moment, whatever it was, has a benefit inside of it waiting to be explored, found and realized.

Take Action

In the song you just watched, there were many moments realized. Right now, I want you to think about a moment in which you would compare to the phrase "days in the sun."

What was that moment and why did you feel like the phrase "days in the sun" applied?

_____

_____

_____

_____

_____

_____

_____

_____

_____

_____

_____

_____

_____

_____

_____

_____

_____

_____

Day 12

**"I've had my moments, days in the sun
Moments I was second to none…
Moments when I knew I did what I thought I
couldn't do."**

Emerson Drive, *Moments*

What would your life be like if you lived in the state of events that were considered "days in the sun"? What would be different for you, your business, your life, your family?

I am pretty sure you would think, feel and act differently. Imagine, waking up with a feeling of a "days in the sun" moment. Now consider a moment in which you felt you were "second to none." A time in which you felt invincible, playing at the top of your game. What about a time in which you felt you had the Midas touch? Where everything you touched turned to gold. Maybe a time in which everything seemed to be going right.

I can hear many saying right now, "Bob, I have never felt that way, I have always had problems and challenges, etc.," I know that is what you may think, but I guarantee that you have had those moments. Examine those moments!

Take Action

Close your eyes and focus on that moment in which you felt "second to none." Identify it and share it with someone today. Ask them about theirs as well. Look into that moment and share it here on the blog, what made

that moment stand out as the one in which you felt
"second to none"?

_____

_____

_____

_____

_____

_____

_____

_____

_____

_____

_____

_____

_____

_____

_____

_____

_____

Day 13

"I've had my moments, days in the sun Moments I was second to none... Moments when I knew I did what I thought I couldn't do."

Emerson Drive, *Moments*

Did you do it? I hope so, because as we draw near to the end of the week you will find out new things about yourself, your moments, and your life.

What happened when someone shared with you about their moments? What did you find interesting about the moments they shared with you? Did the moment seem as monumental to you as it did to them? Realize that it is the moments surrounding the moment that created the power in that moment. That is why you can hear something over and over again and upon hearing it for the hundredth time, it stands out. Because the moments surrounding the "moment" were framing it exactly the way it needed to be in order to be understood.

Take Action

Identify a moment that was so strong for you because of the context of your life at that time. What were the moments that led up to "THE MOMENT"?

_____

_____

_____

_____

_____

_____

_____

_____

_____

_____

_____

_____

_____

_____

_____

_____

_____

_____

Day 14

**"I've had my moments, days in the sun
Moments I was second to none…
Moments when I knew I did what I thought I
couldn't do."**

Emerson Drive, *Moments*

By now you should be becoming more and more aware of the moments of your life. It is one moment leading to another which leads to another that makes up our lives. When someone says, "I saw my life flash before my eyes," do you think that they say a flash of 60-70-80 years all at one time or do you imagine that they saw those "moments" in their lives that meant the most during their lifetime? I see it as the latter.

Now the question is, does a moment happen or can it be created? Well, a moment of time happens whether we are present to it or not. However, the creating of and benefit from particular types of moments is within our control.

For example: when a child does something wrong, the parent can create a "teachable moment" for the child. When disaster strikes, a community can rally and create a moment of generosity. We create moments by our design, or we live in the design of moments as they come to us. The choice is ours. I would rather live by design rather than by infliction, how about you?

Take Action

Today, while living your life, look for a moment in which your response to it might be one way, and choose to respond in a different way. Create your own moment.

_____

_____

_____

_____

_____

_____

_____

_____

_____

_____

_____

_____

_____

_____

_____

_____

_____

Day 15

"I've had my moments, days in the sun
Moments I was second to none...
Moments when I knew I did what I thought I
couldn't do."

Emerson Drive, *Moments*

How many moments have you lived this week? Have they been moments designed by you or moments simply lived by default? Were you able to create moments for yourself? I am confident that if you were living moments by design you created many this week.

Take Action

Make a list of the moments created and enjoyed by you this week.

_____

_____

_____

_____

_____

_____

_____

_____

_____

_____

_____

_____

_____

_____

_____

_____

_____

_____

_____

BOB DONNELL

Week 4

"Good is the enemy of Great."

Jim Collins

Day 16

"Good is the enemy of Great."
Jim Collins

In all of my coaching and dealing with people, I have never heard anyone say, "I want to be good." When asked, almost everyone says that they want to be great. In this statement I believe we find a secret that lets us know how to get great results. Do you see it? Look very closely at the words. One thing I have found is that when enough emotion is evoked towards something, things begin to happen.

If good is normally perceived by most as "good enough," the way to raise the result to great is to come to the realization that good is NOT good enough, but instead, it is the enemy!

Very few people like being told what to do, nor do they like just being (or having) average. They might settle for average, but most want more than that.

Realize today that GOOD is an enemy. Once this is done, you can move from the place that it is no longer tolerable or acceptable and you will begin to raise your standards and increase your results.

Take Action

Greater results always come as a result of having the

ability to look at what you believe in black and white, so take the time to respond to this email!

Describe in detail what you would do if someone were to come into your house while you were there and were going to take something of extreme value to you. Now compare that to how easily you have been willing to handover GREAT results in exchange for GOOD results.

What can you do today in order to show that GOOD is not good enough anymore and that GREAT is the only acceptable way to live your life, love your kids, do your business, deal with clients, meet people on the street, etc.?

_____

_____

_____

_____

_____

_____

_____

_____

_____

_____

Day 17

"Good is the enemy of Great."
Jim Collins

Wow! Incredible responses! Some were very serious about the example. I am confident that many things will change for several people as a result of this exercise.

When placed in the framework of your mind that GOOD is not good enough and we shift our thinking to desiring and pursuing GREAT with all out abandonment, the result will be more things will be done great than would have been done before!

In the illustration of someone coming in and taking a prized possession, many took it quite literally and were ready to defend (especially when it came to a loved one). I am a believer that in this case the loved one we need to consider is YOU individually. When GREAT is the desired outcome, there will be a couple of things that will need to be taken into consideration, let's look at one of them.

Take Action

You will need to consider what the benefits of the desired outcome will be for you, your family, your community, etc. Reply with how living your life to be GREAT rather than good will benefit:

- You

- Your family

- Your friends
- Your company
- Your clients
- Your community

_____

_____

_____

_____

_____

_____

_____

_____

_____

_____

_____

_____

_____

_____

Day 18

"Good is the enemy of Great."
Jim Collins

Some excellent responses. I am always so impressed by the depth of this group and the desire of the members to want to grow! Give yourselves a hand for being part of such a dynamic and vibrant group of people that are changing offices, households, businesses, communities and the world into a better place to be!

The difference between GOOD and GREAT is a great thing to realize. Think about the Olympics. While most remember who won a gold in a particular event, very few (other than friends and family members) will remember who took home the silver or bronze. This does not mean to say that it was not important or not a tremendous achievement. It is just illustrating that one is held in a higher esteem. The difference between GOOD and GREAT is that one is held in a higher esteem.

If you took the athletes placing gold and silver and asked if they would like to change places, you know what the answer would be. So if we have the choice between silver and gold in our lives, why would anyone choose silver? (Please remember that this only a metaphor, I am a believer that whomever is giving 100% of their gifts, talents and resources is achieving gold no matter what.)

Take Action

Look up the two terms.

Good   Great

Decide which one is the one that you want to be known for by:

- Your family

- Your friends

- Your spouse

- Your business

- Your clients

- Your community

- Your country

- Your world

_____

_____

_____

_____

_____

_____

_____

_____

Day 19

"Good is the enemy of Great."
Jim Collins

I am so impressed by some of the commitments that many of you are making to BE GREAT! Congratulations! You rock!

So, the benefits were numerous of living our lives in a great way. It was interesting how people viewed the difference between GOOD and GREAT and how by looking up those words, so many people decided that being GREAT was so superior to just being GOOD.

What is the difference between GOOD and GREAT? Well, what is the difference between first and second, gold or silver medals? It might be 1/10 of a second or 1/10th of a point. It sometimes does not require much more to be great or first than it does to be good or second. The difference can actually be minuscule, but the return can be astronomical!

Take Action

If you have chosen Great as your model, do this:

Explain what great looks like to you in words. The best way to do this in my opinion, is to take out a couple of magazines or surf the web and look for people, things, symbols, ideas, words etc. that create an image of GREAT in your mind.

Now cut them out and put them in a scrapbook or binder or paste them to a board that you can reflect on easily.

_____

_____

_____

_____

_____

_____

_____

_____

_____

_____

_____

_____

_____

_____

_____

Day 20

"Good is the enemy of Great."
Jim Collins

Well? Did you do it? Did you actually go and look for images, words, etc. that helped you paint a mental picture of GREAT? If you did, I know that you are closer to your greatness than you were before you began the exercise. Congratulations!

If you didn't, why not? It is the simple things that we do that can often separate us from the greatness that resides in us. What is holding you back? Do it now! Jim Collins wrote an awesome book, **Good to Great**. The book is worth the cost just to read the first line, which states, "Good is the enemy of great."

Take Action

Identify and reply with how being great versus being good is changing your life, your business, your family, your relationships, etc. Write it as if it is already in the process of happening, because it is. Get the book and read it. It will serve you well in being great!

_____

_____

_____

_____

_____

_____

_____

_____

_____

_____

_____

_____

_____

_____

_____

_____

_____

BOB DONNELL

Week 5

"In essence, if we want to direct our lives, we must take control of our consistent actions. It's not what we do once in a while that shapes our lives, but what we do consistently."

Day 21

"In essence, if we want to direct our lives, we must take control of our consistent actions. It's not what we do once in a while that shapes our lives, but what we do consistently."

Anthony Robbins

The direction of our lives has more to do with the actions we take than it does with the actions that are forced upon us. What actions do you take consistently? I will bet you that those actions get you a particular result. If we really want to take control, we need to be constantly aware of our consistent actions.

Take Action

Consistently monitor our attitude

Consistently plan our day

Consistently adhere to a plan

_____

_____

_____

_____

_____

_____

_____

_____

_____

_____

_____

_____

_____

_____

_____

_____

_____

_____

Day 22

"In essence, if we want to direct our lives, we must take control of our consistent actions. It's not what we do once in a while that shapes our lives, but what we do consistently."

Anthony Robbins

The first step is to decide that we want to direct our lives. I am firmly convinced that many people do not want to direct their lives, for a variety of reasons.

1) That way they don't have to take responsibility for what happens.

1) So that they can always be in a state of chaos (some people love chaos and actually thrive on it).

1) Because they are lazy. They would rather take things as they come than to make the effort required to plan and make something happen a particular way. Do you want to direct your life? If you are enrolled in this program, I believe you do. And if that is true then there will be a series of events that you must do in order to take back control.

Take Action

Make a firm decision in your mind that you want to take back control of your life.

Write out the following, keep it with you, or post it in several places.

Today, __(date)__ , I __(name)__ have decided to take back my own life. I will no longer allow circumstances, events, or others dictate my life to me. From this day forward, my attitude and my actions will be controlled by me and I will begin to take consistent actions toward becoming the person that I was intended to be.

_____

_____

_____

_____

_____

_____

_____

_____

_____

_____

_____

_____

_____

_____

_____

_____

Day 23

"In essence, if we want to direct our lives, we must take control of our consistent actions. It's not what we do once in a while that shapes our lives, but what we do consistently."

Anthony Robbins

Once we have decided to take control of our lives, we must then take control of our consistent actions. As we discussed before, consistent actions form habits and consistent direction wears down a path. What consistent actions have you decided to control? Prospecting, administration, time blocking, spending more time with friends, family, more time on personal development-whatever the consistent actions are that you want to take control of, do it.

Take Action

Make a list of consistent actions which you know will produce the results you want in the following areas:

Family

Spiritual

Physical fitness

Business

Personal development

Now, begin by taking even a small action each day

to change the direction and take back control of the direction in the area.

Make sure to give feedback, in doing so, you cement the process into your mind and life.

_____

_____

_____

_____

_____

_____

_____

_____

_____

_____

_____

_____

_____

_____

_____

Day 24

"In essence, if we want to direct our lives, we must take control of our consistent actions. It's not what we do once in a while that shapes our lives, but what we do consistently."

Anthony Robbins

I sometimes think that people get the word "take" confused with the words "ask for." Once given up, ground is more difficult to gain back. Ask any country that has given land up and then wanted it back. We must be willing to fight for control of our lives once we have given it up. We have to be determined and be diligent to make sure that we are consistent and persistent about reclaiming it.

Take Action

Today's exercise takes action on yesterday's. Today, look at the list of consistent actions that you made and see how many actions you took yesterday. This is not to make you feel bad about it if you didn't take any, but rather to help you focus on growth. No matter how many you did take yesterday, place an increase of 2 more for your action list today. So if you took 3 action steps yesterday, take 5 today. Growth is growth. Just take actions towards growing.

_____

_____

_____

_____

_____

_____

_____

_____

_____

_____

_____

_____

_____

_____

_____

_____

_____

_____

_____

Day 25

"In essence, if we want to direct our lives, we must take control of our consistent actions. It's not what we do once in a while that shapes our lives, but what we do consistently."

Anthony Robbins

What consistent actions did you take this week? Did you define any consistent actions that were lacking in your day? What were they?

Over the course of this exercise you should have been finding it more evident what actions were lacking consistencies. It will become clearer as to the actions that need more consistency and then it is up to you to make a consistent and persistent effort in them.

Remember, the actions that will shape our lives will be the one's done consistently. Good or bad.

Take Action

Today make a list of those actions that you noted as ones you needed to take more seriously and make more consistent. Only the ones that you took some action on this week.

Also type out and reply back to the blog with the quote. Do not copy and paste, Take the 30 seconds and type it out and email it back to me with the list of consistent actions which you took action on this week.

_____

_____

_____

_____

_____

_____

_____

_____

_____

_____

_____

_____

_____

_____

_____

_____

_____

_____

_____

Week 6

"She died from a simple Staph infection.

That, and a few bad decisions."

Dr. House
from the TV show *House*

Day 26

"She died from a simple Staph infection. That, and a few bad decisions."

Dr. House, from the TV show *House*

This episode dealt with a young lady that came in with a medical condition that went undetected. They knew there was a problem, they just couldn't pinpoint it. After a series of tests and misdiagnoses, she died. Right before she died it was determined that it was a simple staph infection that could have been easily treated if it had been diagnosed correctly. Instead all the testing and treatments that were tried eventually weakened the immune system to the point of no return and she died.

Whatever your business looks like today, flourishing or dying, there are two things that will be critical in helping you save it and/or make it the type of business you were designed to have: **Prospecting & Follow-up.**

We do not need doctors, tests, diagnosis, more information, or someone to tell us what to do, the answer is...

☐ Get out

☐ Meet people

☐ Ask the right questions

☐ Follow-up with those people

Take Action

Determine how many people you want to meet today. Don't wait to see how many people you will meet, determine in your mind right now and write it down.

I will meet _____ new people today. I will do this by a series of actions which I will take.

Also write down how you will meet these people. For instance:

- Errands with a purpose

Make a list of the errands you will run today and decide on a number of people you will meet during each errand (make it fun)

- Phone calls

- Attend local events (networking)

- Ask for referrals from past clients and/or existing clients and get in touch with them.

_____

_____

_____

_____

_____

_____

Day 27

"She died from a simple Staph infection. That, and a few bad decisions."

Dr. House, from the TV show *House*

Sometimes the simplest of things can have dramatic consequences.

Things like:

Time management

Attitude

Being fully committed

Rest, relaxation

Personal development

Database management

Exercise

Spending time with friends and family

Follow-up and many others

Take Action

What little things are you doing or not doing that if left unchecked could have severe consequences? List the ones that are going unchecked and send it back to me. Have a great day.

_____

_____

_____

_____

_____

_____

_____

_____

_____

_____

_____

_____

_____

_____

_____

_____

_____

_____

Day 28

"She died from a simple Staph infection. That, and a few bad decisions."

Dr. House, from the TV show *House*

Many people shared several things that were going unchecked. Now here is the tricky part. Just like the patient in the above mentioned episode, getting it checked is critical, but if misdiagnosed, even a simple infection can be deadly. So let me challenge you: many times we misdiagnose what is ailing our business and our lives. Look at the following examples of how we treat our ailment when we are feeling bad about things in general: we feel bad so ...

We eat

We shop

We take the day off

We avoid people

Often rather than correcting what is making us feel bad: our finances, our lack of organization, our physical appearance, etc., we look for something that will make us feel better (even if for a brief moment).

In business, this happens all of the time. It can be recognized behind the disguise of such statements as:

I'll do 'x'...

When I get some more information

When I have more marketing materials

After school ends

After school starts

When I am feeling better

When my spouse becomes more supportive, etc.

Take Action

Look internally to responsibly diagnose what is TRULY ailing you and/or your business. Then take one step today to take the medicine!

The best remedy for the ailment of procrastination is to do it now. The best remedy for fear is to FACE IT! The best remedy for laziness is to exercise.

Take one step in the right direction today and you will begin to feel better and it won't be because of a Band-Aid, but rather because of something that is truly cleaning up the infection!

_____

_____

_____

_____

_____

_____

_____

Day 29

"She died from a simple Staph infection. That, and a few bad decisions."

Dr. House, from the TV show *House*

In the above episode, the patient died due to misdiagnosis and wrong treatments from the doctors. Most often our businesses die due to our bad decisions, not the decisions of others. Here are just a few of the bad decisions that we sometimes make:

Meet someone and do not ask for information to follow-up with them

Get information on someone and do not put them in our database

Put someone in our database and yet do not have any systems in place for effective follow-up

Someone says that they are think they might have the need for our service in a few months, and we simply do not follow-up

Forget to ask for referrals during and after the transaction

Ignore the experience and advice of people who have "been there, done that before."

Try to re-invent the wheel

Take a short cut due to laziness

Believe that being in the office, means that we are working

Spend good "contacting time" 9-5 on tasks which do not require interaction with people (mailing, stuffing envelopes, reading emails, sending out newsletters)

Designing stuff, etc.

The list goes on and on.

Take Action

Look at the above list and pick one or two areas where you have noted a deficiency and take action today to correct it. Even if it is a small step, it will be worth it.

_____

_____

_____

_____

_____

_____

_____

_____

_____

_____

_____

_____

Day 30

"She died from a simple Staph infection. That, and a few bad decisions."

Dr. House, from the TV show *House*

Well, the end of the week is here! Did you pick at least a couple of things this week to change in how you are thinking about and doing things? I know many of you did, because I got some great responses. Thank you.

Were you able to identify the ailment(s) in your life/business? Did you determine what the proper treatment was? Did you ask for help? Did you take the prescription, get it filled and take the medicine?

What items did you choose, and take action on? Tell me what specific actions you took and then tell me what the results were. Maybe the action was small and you think insignificant because it didn't result in a closed sale or something like that, but I assure you that even baby steps in the right direction result in progress!

Make sure that you keep your response to this as you will be able to look back on it later and reflect on your progress!

ABOUT THE AUTHOR

In the growing world of personal development and strategic coaching, few people are as well respected and adored as Bob Donnell. Combining a heart-centered authenticity with winning strategies for business and life, Bob has separated himself as a true leader in the industry. An author, a speaker, and a trainer are just some of the titles he wears boldly. His most important are those of father, humanitarian, connector and Christian!

Having cultivated an entrepreneurial spirit at an early age, he started his first non-profit organization at 18 that focused on helping at-risk families in crisis. Bob has made it his passion and life to study human behavior so as to be able to help even more people by understanding why some do and some don't get the results they truly want.

He realized that the training he received in the area of suicide prevention and crisis intervention was extremely valuable in areas of business as well. He developed a program called **The Art of Intervention**. If the skill set can help someone go from "I want to die" to "I want to live" then it can be used to help a salesperson take a prospect resistant to buying to wanting to buy. This program has proven to be invaluable to salespeople, parents, leaders, coaches, etc. who want to help others have breakthroughs and get outrageous results!

From there, Bob made an impact in the world of sales and in management until he decided to devote the entirety of his life to helping others in transformation.

Programs which have been instrumental in helping business and professionals include: **The Art of Intervention**, **CONNECTOLOGY:** How to Connect With Anyone, Anywhere, Anytime!, **Get The How Out Of The Way, Create A Winning Inner Game,** and others!

That road, however, wasn't arrived at easily. From growing up in poverty to never knowing his father; from the untimely loss of his mother during his teen years to tragically losing his 3 year-old daughter in a freakish car accident, Bob decided that life is too short to continue struggling. He has since devoted his life and business to helping others design their life by getting the results they've been wanting to see.

Now, as a leading Results Strategist, Bob continues to work with entrepreneurs, sales professionals, celebrities, professional athletes as well as any who desires to take their life and business to the next level.

Bob's body of work includes authoring several books, E-books, recording audio programs, hosting radio programs, and currently hosts a weekly live video-streaming, interactive program with members worldwide.

Bob has worked with a distinguished list of companies and clients including Coldwell Banker, Long Beach Grand Prix, Arbonne International, ReMax, World Ventures, Oakley Inc., Pre-Paid Legal. In addition, Bob has loved working within the entertainment industry; the Academy Awards, the WB Music Awards, Victor Awards, The Grammy's and, as a result, has been able to interact with and study some of the great artists in the world including Garth Brooks, The Backstreet Boys, and Will Smith just to mention a few.

The culmination of Bob's 25+ year career has led him to create **Next Level Live** which continues to stand as a beacon for those desperately looking to take their lives to the Next Level. His expertise in knowing the human condition and the keys to getting stronger, faster results sets him apart from his peers.